# Fabulous Friendship Bracelets

This edition published in 2014
By SpiceBox™
12171 Horseshoe Way
Richmond, BC
Canada V7A 4V4

First published in 2007
Copyright © **SpiceBox™** 2007

**ISBN 10:** 1-77132-188-1
**ISBN 13:** 978-1-77132-188-4

CEO & Publisher: Ben Lotfi
Editorial: Trisha Pope, Ania Jaraczewski
Creative Director: Garett Chan
Art Director: Christine Covert
Design, Layout & Illustration: Charmaine Muzyka
Production: James Badger, Mell D'Clute
Sourcing: Janny Lam, Sherry Xie
Photography: Garett Chan, James Badger, Charmaine Muzyka
Special thanks to the models: Cristina Soares, Renee Lawless, Jorgina Thompson,
Jamie Lacamell, Kelly Chan and Claudia Chan

For more SpiceBox products and information, visit our website:
**www.spiceboxbooks.com**

Manufactured in China

3 5 7 9 10 8 6 4 2

# Table of Contents

# Introduction

Friendship bracelets are a great way to share your fashion sense with friends! These fabulous accessories are easy to make, and you can pick any design and colors you want to express your style. Invite some friends over for a day of bracelet-making fun, and then exchange your creations with each other!

There is a great tradition that you can follow when you give a bracelet to a friend: Tell your friend to make a wish as you tie the bracelet onto their wrist. If your friend wears the bracelet until it's worn out and falls off their wrist by itself, the wish should come true!

When you make a bracelet for someone, you can use their favorite colors, or you can pick out colors that match their personality. Check out this list to see which colors would be perfect for your friend:

Red – energetic

Orange – adventurous

Green – responsible

Yellow – cheerful

Blue – loyal

Purple – creative

Pink – playful

Black – strong

Brown – friendly

Gray – smart

White – calm

# Getting Started

One of the things that has helped friendship bracelets maintain their popularity for more than thirty years is that you can achieve eye-catching results with very few supplies. Also, the techniques are straightforward and easy to learn.

You will learn how to create cool friendship bracelets using the wheel and square loom that are in your kit. They are simple to make as long as you follow the pattern templates and the instructions, and they are so cute! We'll also show you how to make the traditional friendship bracelets that are based on a series of knots. Patterns for the traditional bracelets start out from very basic ones, to ones that are quite complex. If you've never made a friendship bracelet before, we recommend that you start right at the beginning with the very first bracelet and work your way through to the harder ones. But first, let's look at the materials in the kit as well as some basic instructions.

## Did you know?

The origin of friendship bracelets is most likely Central American countries where they are a traditional handicraft. They only became popular in North America in the 1970s, but have remained popular ever since.

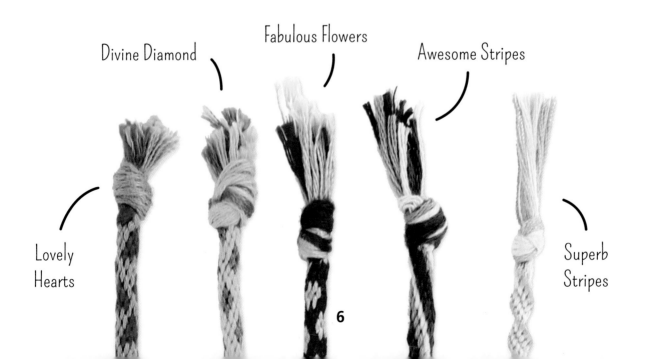

Divine Diamond

Fabulous Flowers

Awesome Stripes

Lovely Hearts

Superb Stripes

# Tools & Supplies

**Threads:** Regular 6-strand embroidery floss is the most popular type of thread used to make friendship bracelets. It comes in an amazing range of colors, including glittery and neon threads! It's not the only material you can use, though. You could make a friendship bracelet with any lightweight yarn or string that will hold a knot, and there are lots of fun yarns you can find in a craft or hobby store to experiment with. Remember that the thicker the threads, the chunkier the bracelet will be.

**Safety pins/tape:** The easiest way to secure the traditional style of knotted bracelets while you are working is to tape the loose ends to your table or to pin the knot onto the leg of your jeans or to your bed.

**Beads:** Fun, colorful beads will make your bracelets even more eye-catching. See page 11 for tips on how to use beads in your bracelets. It's easy to do!

**Friendship bracelet makers and templates:** The friendship bracelet wheel and square loom come in 3 pieces: the foam base, the pattern templates and the clear cover. The foam base is notched all the way around, has 4 small holes and one large one in the center. The holes in the templates need to line up with the holes in the wheel/loom. Once they do, press the 4 knobs on the plastic cover into the holes to keep the template in place. Instructions for how to use the wheel are on pages 13–21, and the square loom instructions are on pages 49–53.

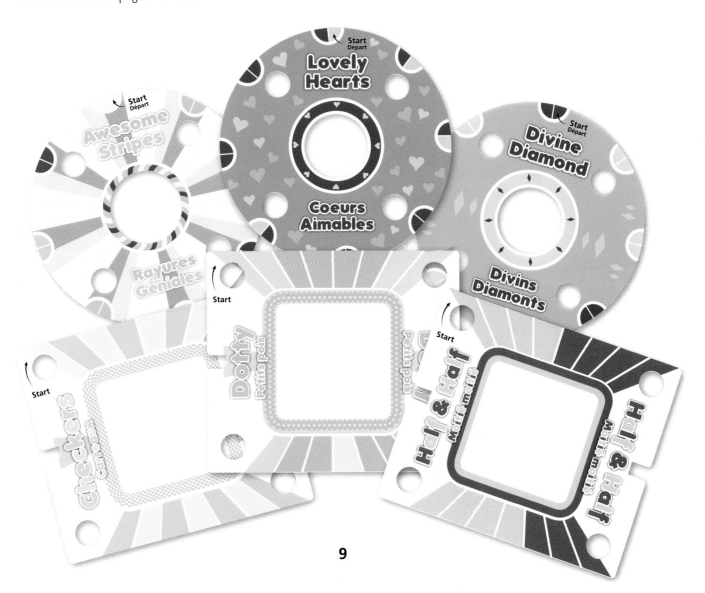

9

# Starting & Finishing Your Bracelets

Each bracelet pattern shows you how long your threads should be and how many threads of each color you will need to cut. Every bracelet starts with tying all the threads together, but there are different ways you can do this depending on which style you like best.

## Bracelet Length

To make your bracelet the right length, measure your wrist with enough give so that the bracelet will be a bit loose. Then you can use the handy rulers on the pages at the back of the book to measure your work as you go. There's also a log to record the measurements of your wrist and your friends' wrists so you always know how long to make your bracelets.

## Starting with a Loop

This symbol tells you how long to cut the threads if you want to start with a loop.

**1.** Choose the colors you want, then measure out and cut the number of strings shown on the chart at the beginning of the pattern.

**2.** Group the strings all together and lay them out flat.

**3.** Fold the whole bundle of strings in half over a felt marker.

**4.** Tie the strings together into a knot, pulling the knot up tight to the marker. Take out the marker and you'll have a loop.

**5.** Follow the bracelet pattern until you have reached the length you measured out earlier.

**6.** Create 2 braids with the loose string at the end of the bracelet (see page 12). Now you can thread one of the braids through the loop you made at the beginning of your bracelet and then tie it together with the other braid to fasten your bracelet.

## Starting with a Knot

This symbol tells you how long to cut the threads if you want to start with a knot.

**1.** Choose the colors you want, then measure out and cut the number of strings shown on the chart at the beginning of the pattern.

**2.** Hold the strings together and tie the ends into a knot, leaving about 3 inches (7 cm) of loose string.

**3.** Follow the bracelet pattern until you have reached the length you measured out earlier.

**4.** To finish, tie another knot at the end of your bracelet. Leave about 3 inches (7 cm) of loose thread and trim the ends.

## Adding Beads

Inside your kit you'll find lots of fun beads that you can add to your bracelet. Some of the patterns will tell you specifically how to thread beads onto the bracelet you're working on, but you can add beads to any of the bracelets you make. Here are a few techniques you can use:

**1.** When you finish off the ends of your bracelets, you can thread beads onto the loose strings and secure them with knots. This will give your bracelet a cute dangling charm effect.

**2.** If you are finishing with braids, tie a knot at the end of the braid, then thread all of the loose strings through a bead or two, and tie another knot to secure the beads.

**3.** You can add beads in the middle of bracelets too. After a few rows of knotting, thread a bead or two onto the strings, bring them up against the last row of knots, and then continue knotting according to the pattern. This is a great way to personalize the patterns and make them totally unique!

**4.** Finally, you can simply sew a few large beads onto one side of your finished bracelet. Ask an adult to help you with the needle and thread.

# How to make a braid:

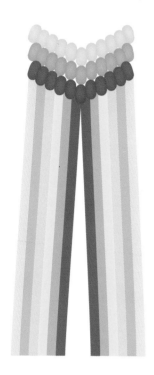

**1.** Split the threads in half down the middle. You will be making a braid with each set of threads.

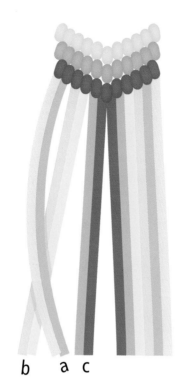

*b a c*

**2.** Take one half of the threads and split them into 3 sections. Pick up the left group of threads (a) and move them between the other two groups (b and c).

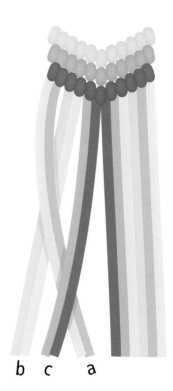

*b c a*

**3.** Now take the right group of threads (c) and move them between the other two groups (a and b).

*b a*  *c*

**4.** Continue braiding in this way, alternating between moving the left and right groups of threads into the middle, until you have about 2 inches (5 cm) of braid, then make a knot at the end. Repeat steps 2–4 with the other half of your bracelet so that you have 2 braids that you can use to tie the bracelet around your wrist.

# Friendship Bracelet Wheel

The friendship bracelet wheel is a cool way to make fabulous friendship bracelets. You will want to make plenty of these bracelets to give to your whole circle of friends. They are going to love them!

There are 5 different pattern templates you can use with the wheels, and we have included 2 of each design in different color combinations. Use the colors on the templates to start, and then once you get the hang of it, experiment with your own color combinations.

# Setting Up the Bracelet Wheel

Scan this code to watch an online video on how to use the wheel!

## Preparing Your Threads

Look at your pattern template and select strings to match the colors on the tabs. For each color tab, you will need one string in that color. See pages 10–11 for tips on how to get your threads ready for knotting.

|  | 40 in/100 cm | 20 in/50 cm |
|---|---|---|
| Yellow | 2 | 4 |
| Blue | 2 | 4 |
| Purple | 2 | 4 |
| Pink or green | 2 | 4 |

14

Setting up the bracelet wheel properly is the first step. Whichever pattern you choose, you will need to set up the wheel the same way. Follow these steps carefully to get started.

**1.** Prepare your strings according to the chart on the previous page, referring to the instructions on pages 10–11 for help, if you need it.

**2.** Set your wheel on the table with the START arrow positioned at the top.

**3.** Place your strings so that the knot is in the hole in the middle of the wheel, and the strings are fanned out so that you can pick them up easily.

**4.** Hold the knot down in the center of the wheel with one finger so that it doesn't move, and with your other hand pick up a string and notch it into the wheel in a tab of the same color.

**5.** Continue to hold the knot in place while you position all of the strings into tabs of the matching color. Once they are all in place, pick up the wheel and adjust any strings that are loose. Your wheel is now set up and you can start making bracelets!

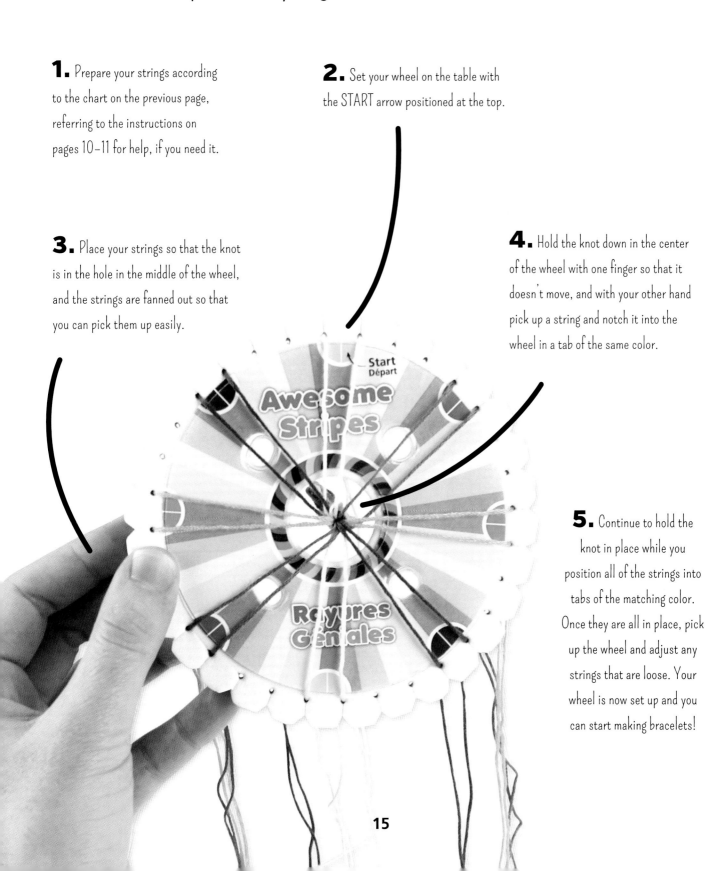

# Awesome Stripes

Follow each step carefully for a few rounds. Once you get the hang of it you'll see how quick and easy it is to make these fab bracelets!

| | 40 in/100 cm | 20 in/50 cm |
|---|---|---|
| Yellow | 2 | 4 |
| Blue | 2 | 4 |
| Purple | 2 | 4 |
| Red or green | 2 | 4 |

**1.** Cut all your threads according to the chart, then set up your wheel following the instructions on pages 14–15. Position your wheel so that the START arrow is at the top.

**2.** There should be 2 yellow strings in the 2 notches at the top of your wheel and 2 at the bottom. Unhook the TOP RIGHT string from the wheel. Move the string to the bottom of the wheel, and hook it into the tab beside the BOTTOM RIGHT string.

16

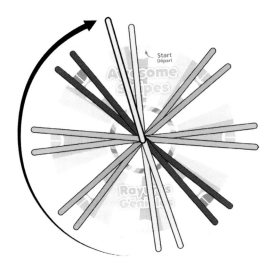

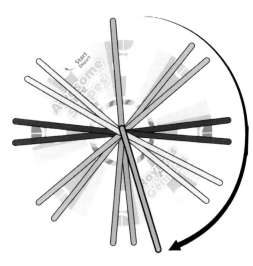

**3.** Unhook the BOTTOM LEFT string and rehook it into the notch to the left of the TOP LEFT string. Check to make sure your wheel now looks like the diagram.

**4.** Turn your wheel counterclockwise, or to the LEFT one tab. The BLUE strings should now be at the top of your wheel. Unhook the TOP RIGHT blue string and hook it back into the wheel beside the BOTTOM RIGHT string.

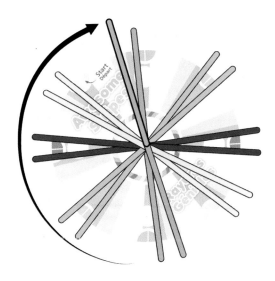

**5.** Unhook the BOTTOM LEFT string and rehook it to the left of the TOP LEFT string.

**6.** Turn the wheel to the left—counterclockwise—until the green strings are at the top. Continue hooking and rehooking your strings in the same way, then move on to the purple strings, and then back to yellow. Watch your bracelet grow!

**To finish:** When your bracelet is long enough, unhook all the strings, being careful not to tangle them up. Tie them in a knot at the bottom and trim the bracelet neatly, making sure you have enough thread to tie it onto your wrist.

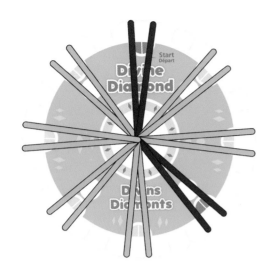

## Divine Diamond

| | 40 in/100 cm | 20 in/50 cm |
|---|---|---|
| Green or orange | 6 | 12 |
| Purple or blue | 2 | 4 |

Follow the same instructions as for the Awesome Stripes bracelet. This time, however, your top 2 notches will have purple strings. To start, you will move the right string to the right of the green tab at the bottom of the wheel. You will then move the left string in the green tab to the left of the purple tab at the top.

## Lovely Hearts

| | 40 in/100 cm | 20 in/50 cm |
|---|---|---|
| Yellow or red | 3 | 6 |
| Purple or mauve | 5 | 10 |

This bracelet is a bit different because some of the tabs have 2 different colors. But don't let this confuse you. Just follow exactly the same instructions for the Awesome Stripes and you will see a pretty bracelet of hearts emerge as you knot!

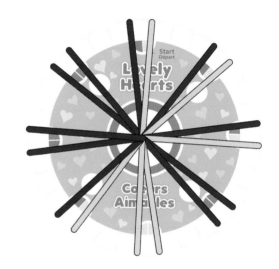

## Fabulous Flower

| | 40 in/100 cm | 20 in/50 cm |
|---|---|---|
| Yellow | n/a | 1 |
| Blue or pink | n/a | 6 |
| Red or blue | n/a | 9 |

The single yellow string creates the center of each flower. The 6 strings are the petals, and the remaining 9 strings make up the background color. After you have made this bracelet once to learn the pattern, choose your own colors and experiment to create different looks. Simply cut the same number of strings in different colors for each tab of the wheel and watch your flowers bloom!

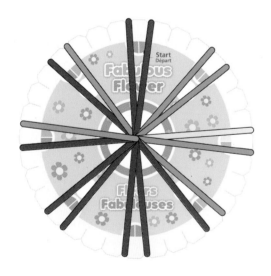

**Tip:** When taking a string off the top, take the thread from the right and replace on the right. When taking a string from the bottom, take from the left and return to the left.

# Superb Stripes

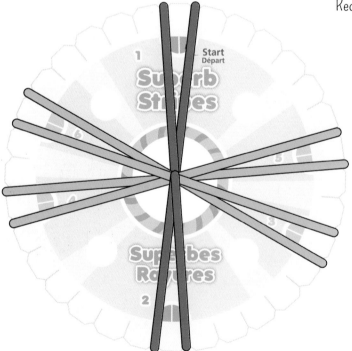

This pattern is a bit different because there are fewer strings and tabs, and you are also not going to spin your wheel as you knot. Start your bracelet in the same way, by cutting and knotting your strings and then stringing them onto the wheel in the correct notches.

| | 40 in/100 cm | 20 in/50 cm |
|---|---|---|
| Dark or light pink | 2 | 4 |
| Red or green | 4 | 8 |

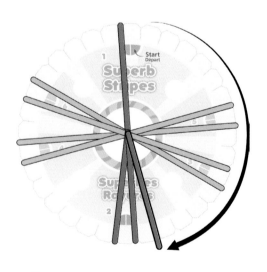

**1.** Unhook the TAB 1 right string and move it to the right of TAB 2.

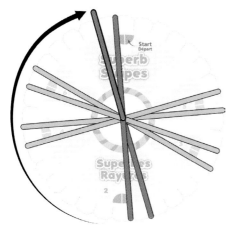

**2.** Unhook the left string of TAB 2 and rehook it to the left of TAB 1.

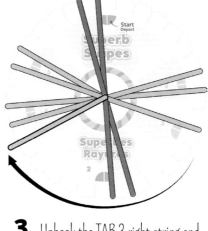

**3.** Unhook the TAB 3 right string and move it to the right notch of TAB 4.

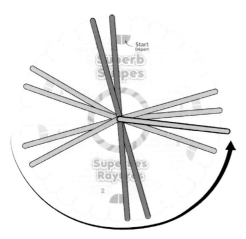

**4.** Unhook the left string of TAB 4 and rehook it to the left of TAB 3.

**5.** Unhook the TAB 5 right string and move it to the right notch of TAB 6.

**6.** Unhook the left string of TAB 6 and rehook it to the left of TAB 5.

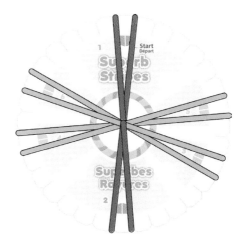

**7.** Move each string CLOCKWISE (to the RIGHT) so that they are lined up on the tabs again. Repeat steps 1–7 until your bracelet is long enough to tie on.

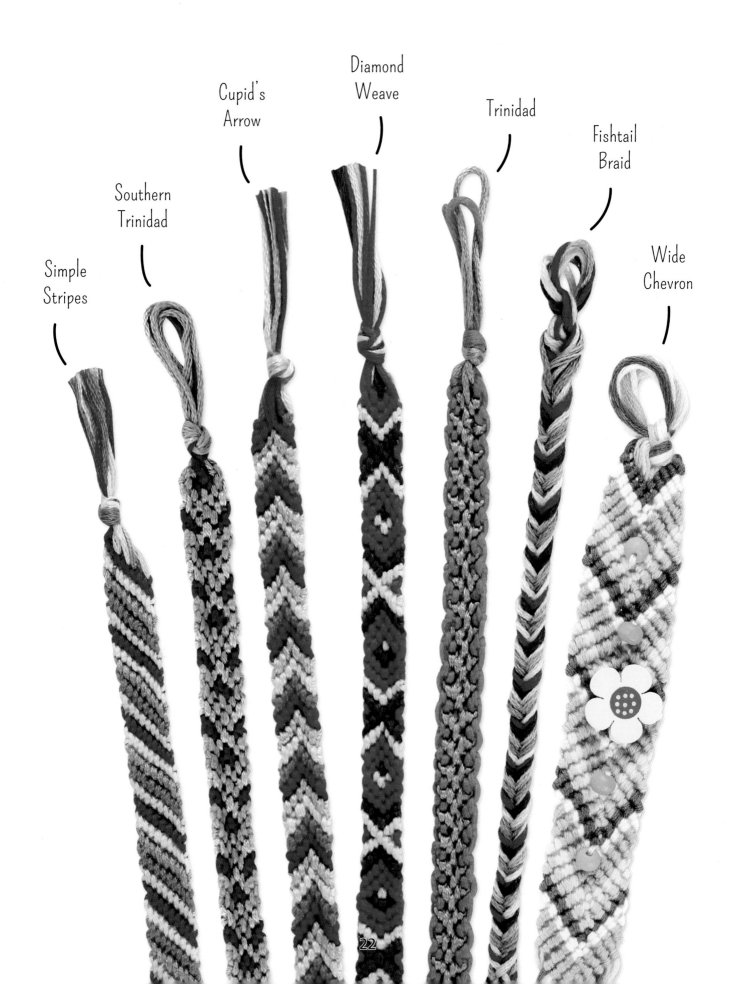

Simple
Stripes

Southern
Trinidad

Cupid's
Arrow

Diamond
Weave

Trinidad

Fishtail
Braid

Wide
Chevron

22

Wrap with Beads

# Hand-woven Bracelets

The next few patterns are for classic hand-knotted bracelets just like the ones that people have been making for centuries. You can give this traditional handicraft a modern twist by looking for embroidery floss in bright, trendy colors, including neon, glittery and metallic threads! Once you've mastered a few basic knotting styles, there is no limit to what you can do, so have a go at designing your own fab bracelet fashions!

Rainbow

# A Basic Knot

In order to make a traditional, knotted friendship bracelet
you need to tie a basic knot in two different directions.

## A Right-loop Knot:

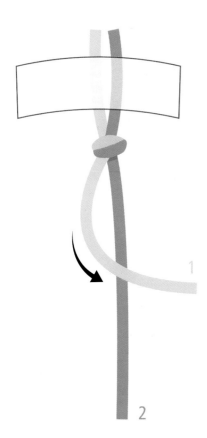 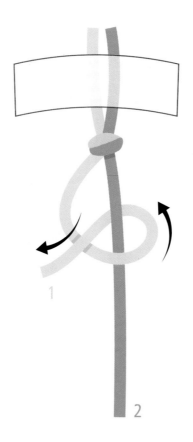 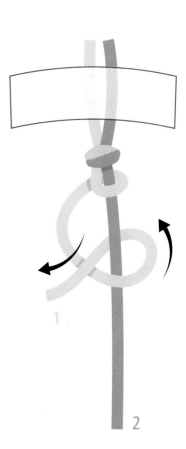

**1.** Knot 2 pieces of thread and tape
them to a surface. Hold the second
string (2) firmly and cross the first
string (1) over it, leaving a loop
like in the diagram.

**2.** Pass the first string (1)
underneath the second string (2)
and up through the loop—pull on it
to make a knot. Slide the knot up
to the top and pull it tight.

**3.** Now, repeat the process in order
to make a double knot. You've made
your first complete right-loop knot!

## A Left-loop Knot:

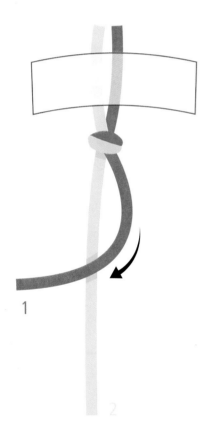

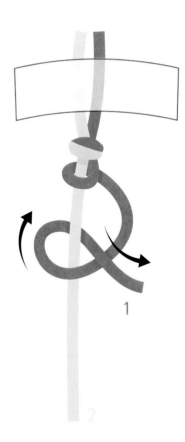

**1.** Knot 2 pieces of thread and tape them to a surface. Hold the second string (2) firmly and cross the first string (1) over it, leaving a loop like in the diagram.

**2.** Send the first string (1) under the second string (2) and up through the loop. Softly pull on it to make a knot. Slide the knot up to the top of the board and pull it tight.

**3.** Now, repeat the process in order to make a double knot. You've made your first complete left-loop knot!

# Simple Stripes

This is a great bracelet to start with because it only uses one type of knot that is repeated over and over. Once you get the hang of it, it's a snap to finish!

28 in/70 cm
6 colors - 1 string per color

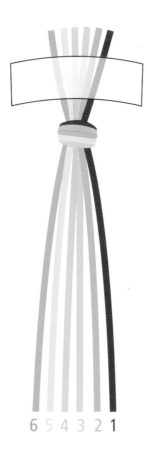

6 5 4 3 2 1

**1.** Tie your strings together and attach them to your work surface. To make it easier the first time, use the same colors of thread in the same order as in the diagram.

6 5 4 3 1 2

**2.** Pick up the string on the far right (string 1) and tie a left-loop knot (see page 25) over string 2. Pull the knot tight.

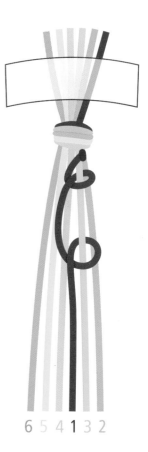

6 5 4 1 3 2

**3.** Still using string 1, tie a left-loop knot over string 3. Remember that you must tie 2 loops for a complete knot.

**1** 6 5 4 3 2        **1** 6 5 4 2 3        2 **1** 6 5 4 3

**4.** Next tie left-loop knots over strings 4, 5 and 6. String 1 should now be to the left of all the other strings.

**5.** Next pick up string 2, which is now the string on the far right. Tie a left-loop knot over string 3, remembering to tie a double knot.

**6.** With string 2, tie left-loop knots over strings 4, 5, 6 and 1. String 2 should now be to the left of all the other strings.

3 2 **1** 6 5 4

**7.** With string 3, tie left-loop knots over strings 4, 5, 6, 1 and 2. Continue this pattern with strings 5 and 6. When you have used all the different colors, string 1 will be on the far right again, and you can repeat the pattern starting at step 2 until your bracelet is the length you want.

Tie the loose ends into a knot, and your bracelet is ready to wear!

27

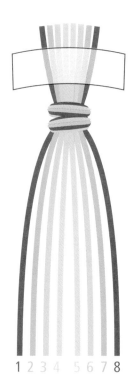

# Cupid's Arrow

For this bracelet, you will take your knotting skills to the next level! Use the left-loop knot and the right-loop knot to make the V-shaped rows, or chevrons.

 60 in/150 cm
4 colors - 1 string per color

 30 in/75 cm
4 colors - 2 strings per color

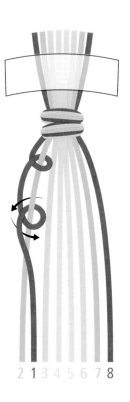

1 2 3 4　5 6 7 8

2 1 3 4 5 6 7 8

2 3 4 1 5 6 7 8

**1.** Choose 4 colors of thread and cut them into the lengths you need. Tie them in a knot and attach them to your work surface.

**2.** Start with string 1 and make a right-loop knot over string 2. Remember to make 2 loops for every knot.

**3.** With string 1, make right-loop knots over strings 3 and 4. String 1 will now be in the middle.

28

2 3 4 **1** 5 6 **8** 7

2 3 4 **1 8** 5 6 7

2 3 4 **8 1** 5 6 7

**4.** Now pick up string 8 and make a left-loop knot over string 7.

**5.** With string 8, make left-loop knots over strings 6 and 5. String 8 will now be beside string 1.

**6.** Take string 1 and make a right-loop knot over string 8. You have completed your first chevron!

**7.** Now take string 2 and make a right-loop knot over string 3. Complete the chevron the same way you made the first one.

**8.** Now make chevrons with the 2 remaining colors. You can see that the order of the colors is now back to how they were in step 1. Repeat steps 2–8 until you have the length of bracelet that you want.

3 2 4 **8 1** 5 6 7

**8** 7 6 5 4 3 2 **1**

# Diamond Weave

This is a more complicated bracelet to make, but with such a cool pattern it's worth the time and effort! Just keep your place in the pattern and keep knotting!

| | |
|---|---|
| ![key icon] **40 in/100 cm** 3 colors - 1 or 2 strings per color (see diagram) | ![scissors icon] **20 in/50 cm** 3 colors - 2 or 4 strings per color (see diagram) |

1 2 3 4 5 6 7 8

2 1 3 4 5 6 7 8

3 4 8 7 2 1 5 6

**1.** Choose 3 colors and cut them to the lengths you need. Tie them in a knot and attach them to your work surface.

**2.** The first 4 rows of knots will be chevrons, as you made in Cupid's Arrow on page 28. Remember how this goes? Start with string 1 and tie right-loop knots over strings 2, 3 and 4.

**3.** Then take string 8 and tie left-loop knots over strings 7, 6 and 5. Now take string 1 and tie a right-loop knot over string 8. Make a second row of the same color with strings 2 and 7.

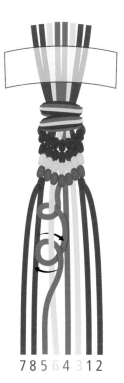

87654321

78654321

78564312

**5.** Make a row with your second color using strings 3 and 6, and a row with the third color using strings 4 and 5. You should have 4 rows altogether, with strings 8 and 1 on the outside again.

**6.** Take string 8 and make a right-loop knot over string 7. On the other side of the bracelet, take string 1 and make a left-loop knot over string 2.

**7.** Now you are going to make the bottom half of the X. Take string 5 and make left-loop knots over strings 6, 8 and 7.

**8.** Take string 4 and make right-loop knots over strings 3, 1 and 2.

**9.** Now you are going to make an upside-down chevron. Take string 6 and make a right-loop knot over string 3. Now take string 3 and make left-loop knots over strings 8, 7 and 5. Then take string 6 and make right-loop knots over strings 1, 2 and 4.

57863124

35781246

# Diamond Weave (con't)

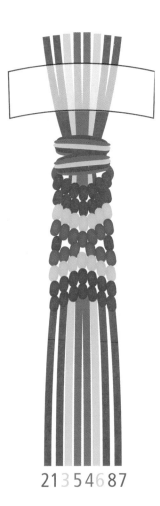

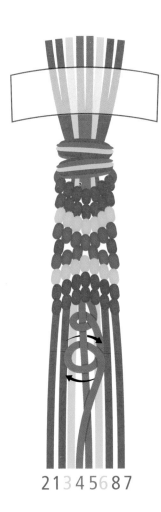

2 1 3 5 4 6 8 7

2 1 3 4 5 6 8 7

2 1 4 3 6 5 8 7

**10.** Make 2 more upside-down chevrons with strings 8 and 1, and strings 7 and 2.

**11.** Take string 4 and make a left-loop knot over string 5.

**12.** Now take string 4 and make a left-loop knot over string 3. Then take string 5 and make a right-loop knot over string 6.

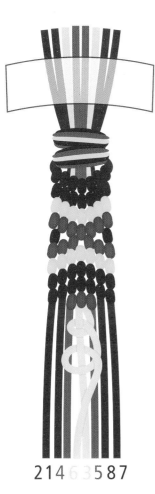

2 1 4 6 3 5 8 7

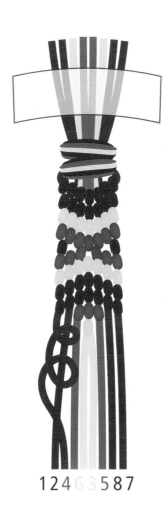

1 2 4 6 3 5 8 7

1 4 6 7 2 3 5 8

**13.** Take string 6 and make a left-loop knot over string 3.

**14.** Take string 2 and make right-loop knots over strings 1, 4 and 6.

**15.** Take string 7 and make left-loop knots over strings 8, 5 and 3. Take string 2 and make a right-loop knot over string 7 to finish the chevron.

To continue the bracelet, make another chevron in the same color, making knots with strings 1 and 8. Then repeat the pattern, starting at step 5. Note that the order of the colors will change in the next section. Look at the illustration to see which color comes next.

# Wide Chevron

This bracelet is very similar to Cupid's Arrow, but is worked with four strings of each color to make it extra wide so you can decorate it with pretty beads.

 70 in/180 cm
6 colors - 2 strings per color

 35 in/90 cm
6 colors - 4 strings per color

**Note:** The diagram only shows 1 string for every 2 strings of thread that you will need. You should have 4 strings for each color: 2 on each side. You will work with each pair of strings as though they are 1 string.

**1.** Choose 6 colors of thread and cut them to the lengths you need. You should have 2 strings for each string in the diagram.

**2.** Take the 2 strings of the same color on the far left (string 1 in the diagram) and make a right-loop knot over both strings of the next color to the right (string 2).

**3.** Continue making right-loop knots with string 1 over strings 3, 4, 5 and 6.

2 3 4 5 6 1 7 8 9 10 12 11

**4.** Take the 2 strings on the far right (string 12) and make a left-loop knot over both strings of the next color to the left (string 11). Continue making left-loop knots with string 12 over strings 10, 9, 8 and 7.

2 3 4 5 6 12 1 7 8 9 10 11

**5.** Take string 1 and make a right-loop knot over string 12 to complete your first chevron.

11 10 9 8 7 1 12 6 5 3 4 2

**6.** Make chevrons with each of the remaining colors the same way you did the first. Continue the pattern until it's long enough to go around your wrist.

## Beading tips:

You can make your bracelet even more stylish by adding some beautiful beads! Simply sew some pretty beads onto your bracelet. Ask an adult for help using a needle and thread.

# Southern Trinidad

With this bracelet, you are knotting the middle strings first, and then the outer ones, which is a little different from what you've done so far.

|  | 64 in/160 cm<br>4 colors - 1 string per color |  | 32 in/80 cm<br>4 colors - 2 strings per color |
|---|---|---|---|

1 2 3 **4 5** 6 7 8

**1.** Choose 4 colors and cut them to the lengths you need. Tie them in a knot and attach them to your work surface.

1 2 3 **5 4** 6 7 8

**2.** Start in the middle. Take string 4 and make a right-loop knot over string 5.

1 2 3 **5** 6 **4** 7 8

**3.** Still using string 4, make a right-loop knot over string 6.

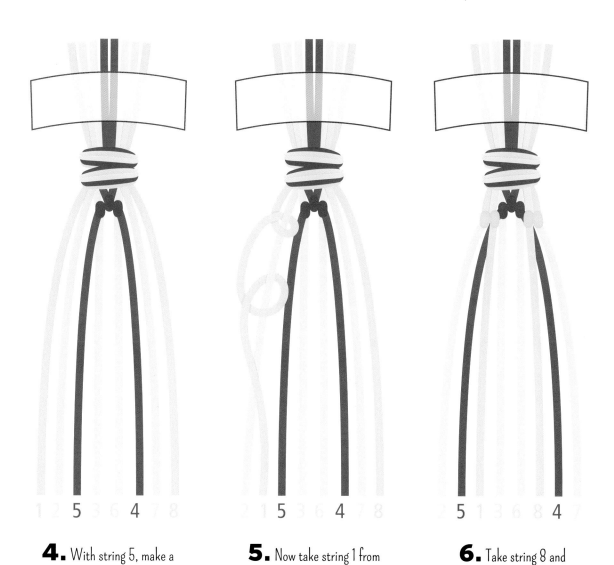

**4.** With string 5, make a left-loop knot over string 3.

**5.** Now take string 1 from the left side of the bracelet and make right-loop knots over strings 2 and 5.

**6.** Take string 8 and make left-loop knots over strings 7 and 4.

**Tip:** Tension refers to how tightly or loosely the threads are knotted. As you become better at making bracelets, try to be consistent in how firmly you tie your knots so that your pattern looks even and pretty.

**7.** Take string 3 and make right-loop knots over string 6 and 8. Then take string 6 and make a left-loop knot over string 1.

**8.** Take string 2 and make right-loop knots over strings 5 and 6. Then take string 7 and make left-loop knots over strings 4 and 3.

**9.** Take string 1 and make right-loop knots over strings 8 and 7. Then take string 8 and make a left-loop knot over string 2.

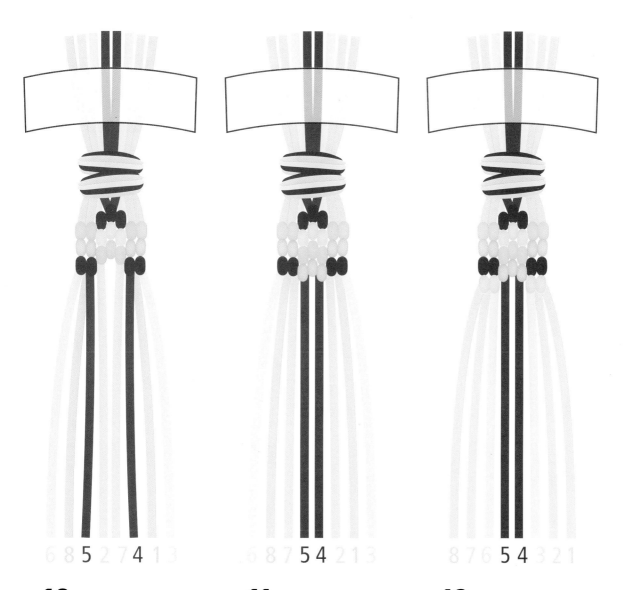

**10.** Take string 5 and make right-loop knots over strings 6 and 8. Then take string 4 and make left-loop knots over strings 3 and 1.

**11.** Take string 2 and make right-loop knots over strings 7 and 4. Then take string 7 and make a left-loop knot over string 5.

**12.** Take string 6 and make right-loop knots over strings 8 and 7. Then take string 3 and make left-loop knots over strings 1 and 2. Repeat from step 1 to finish your bracelet.

# Trinidad

With this bracelet, you will use the technique of skipping knots, which creates an elegant, almost lacy effect.

|  60 in/150 cm<br>2 colors - 2 strings per color |  30 in/75 cm<br>2 colors - 4 strings per color |

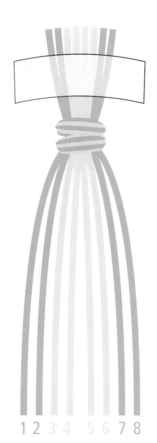

1 2 3 4 5 6 7 8

**1.** Choose 2 colors and cut them to the lengths you need. Tie them in a knot and attach them to your work surface.

1 2 3 4 5 6 7 8

**2.** Take string 1 and make right-loop knots over strings 2 and 3.

2 3 1 4 5 8 6 7

**3.** Take string 8 and make left-loop knots over strings 7 and 6.

40

2 1      8 7         2 1      8 7         2 1      8 7

**4.** Take string 3 and make right-loop knots over strings 1 and 4. Take string 6 and make left-loop knots over 8 and 5.

**5.** Take string 3 and make a right-loop knot over string 6.

**6.** Check the order of your strings: 2 1 4 6 3 5 8 7.

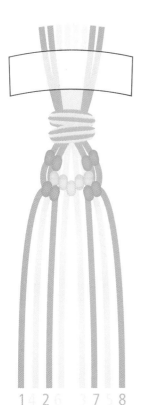

1 4 2 6    3 7 5 8

**7.** Take string 2 and make right-loop knots over strings 1 and 4. Take string 7 and make left-loop knots over strings 8 and 5.

1 2 6 5    4 3 7 8

**8.** Take string 4 and make right-loop knots over strings 2 and 6. Take string 5 and make left-loop knots over 7 and 3. Use string 4 to make a right-loop knot over string 5.

Repeat steps 2–8 until the bracelet is as long as you want, then finish it off. Now it's ready to wear!

# Fishtail Braid

This is a different kind of braid than the one you learned earlier. You can make this with as many or as few colors as you want, so pick out your faves!

| | |
|---|---|
| 50 in/130 cm | 25 in/65 cm |
| 6 colors - 1 string per color | 6 colors - 2 strings per color |

1 2 3 4 5 6 7 8 9 10 11 12

1 2 3 4 5 6    7 8 9 10 11 12

2 3 4 5 6 12    1 7 8 9 10 11

**1.** Choose 6 colors and cut them to the lengths you need. Tie them in a knot and attach them to your work surface.

**2.** Split your strings into 2 sections as shown in the diagram.

**3.** Take strings 1 and 12 from the outsides of the bracelet and cross them over in the middle.

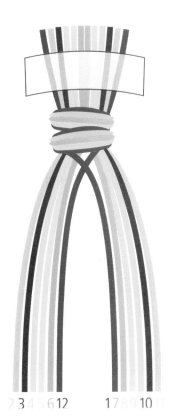

**4.** Pull the strings tight so that the spot where the strings cross is close to the knot.

**5.** Take strings 2 and 11 and cross them over in the middle.

**6.** Pull the strings tight just under strings 1 and 12. Take strings 3 and 10 and cross them over in the middle. Pull the strings tight.

**7.** You will see that a braid is starting to form. Continue taking the 2 outside strings and bringing them into the middle until your braid is as long as you want.

# Rainbow

This bracelet is made from 7 small bracelets tied together at the ends. Or, instead of tying them all together, wear a different color for every day of the week!

|  | 2 strings of 20 in/50 cm<br>1 string of 70 in/180 cm | In each of red, orange, yellow, green, blue, indigo, violet |
|---|---|---|

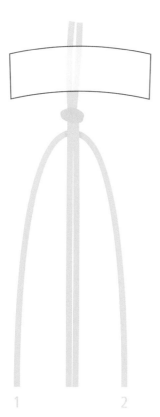

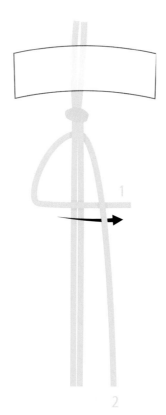

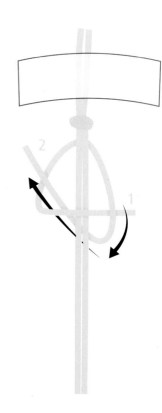

**1.** Using all the strings of one color, tie the 2 shorter strings together, and slide the longer string underneath as shown.

**2.** Take the string on the left side and place it over the 2 middle strings and under the right string, making a loop.

**3.** Now take the right string and slide it under the middle strings and through the loop. Pull the strings tight.

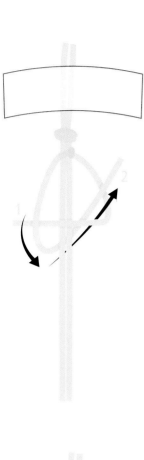

**4.** Now do the reverse: use the right string to create a loop, and take the left string and slide it under the middle strings and though the loop.

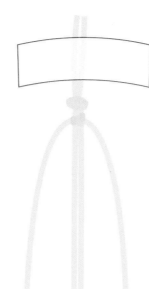

**5.** Pull the strings tight. You have now completed one knot, called a "square knot."

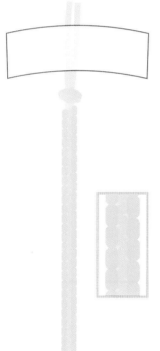

**6.** Continue making square knots until the bracelet is as long as you want, then tie a knot, leaving a few inches loose.

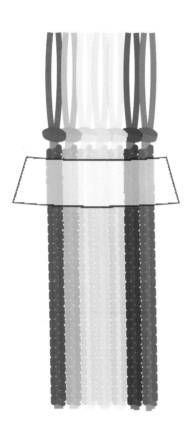

**7.** Make one bracelet in each of the 7 colors. Line them up together and tape them down to your work surface.

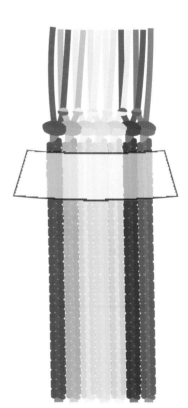

**8.** Using the loose ends, tie a red string to an orange string, an orange string to a yellow string and so on. This will join all your bracelets into one.

# Wrap with Beads

Make this chic beaded bracelet long enough to wrap around your wrist a couple of times. It's quick and easy to make, but super stylish to wear!

| | 35 in/90 cm  3 strings | 15 beads in colors to match your thread |
| --- | --- | --- |

1 2 3

2 1 3

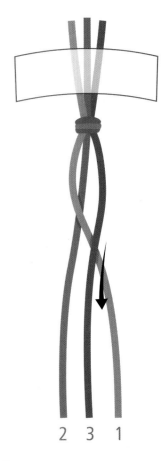

2 3 1

**1.** Cut 3 strings to the lengths you need. Tie them together and attach them to your work surface.

**2.** Take string 1 and place it sugly between strings 2 and 3.

**3.** Take string 3 and place it snugly between strings 2 and 1.

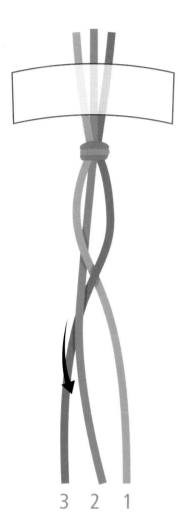

3 2 1

13 2

**4.** Take string 2 and place it snugly between strings 3 and 1.

**5.** Continue braiding by repeating steps 2–4 until the braid is about 1½ inches (4 cm) long. Make a knot.

**6.** Thread 3 beads onto your bracelet, over all 3 threads. Make another knot.

**To finish your bracelet:** Repeat steps 2–6 until the bracelet is long enough to loop around your wrist a couple of times. Make another knot to finish off and cut the threads so you have enough string to tie the ends together.

Dotty

Checkers

Zipper

Half & Half

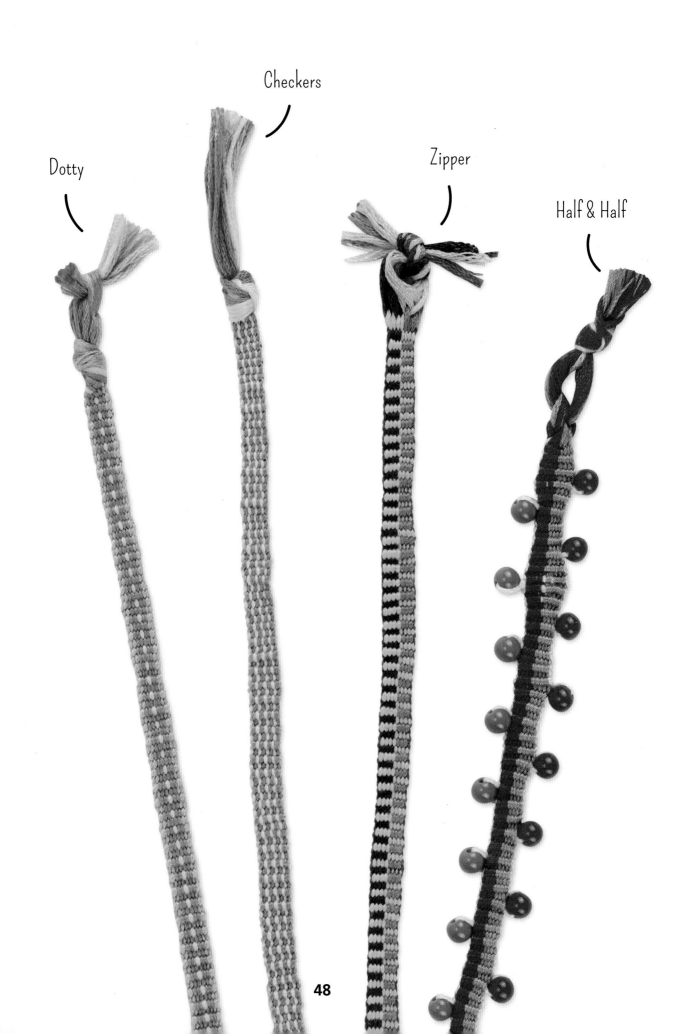

**48**

# How To Use the Square Loom

The square bracelet loom is similar to the wheel, but instead of round woven bracelets, you will get flat bracelets.

### Checkers

| | |
|---|---|
| Yellow | 7 x 20 in/50 cm |
| Blue | 8 x 20 in/50 cm |
| Green | 2 x 40 in/100 cm |

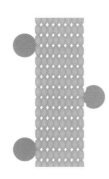 

### Half & Half

| | |
|---|---|
| Purple | 8 x 20 in/50 cm |
| Pink | 7 x 20 in/50 cm |
| White | 2 x 40 in/100 cm |

### Zipper

| | |
|---|---|
| Purple | 4 x 20 in/50 cm |
| Green | 4 x 20 in/50 cm |
| Yellow | 4 x 20 in/50 cm |
| Pink | 2 x 40 in/100 cm |

### Dotty

| | |
|---|---|
| Green | 6 x 20 in/50 cm |
| | 2 x 40 in/100 cm |
| Pink | 8 x 20 in/50 cm |
| Yellow | 1 x 20 in/50 cm |

**1.** Pick a bracelet pattern that you want to use and cut the right number of strings. Leave 3 inches (7.5 cm) loose at the top, and tie a knot. Attach the knot to your work surface.

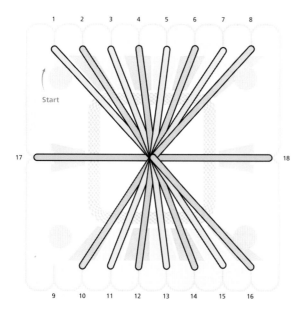

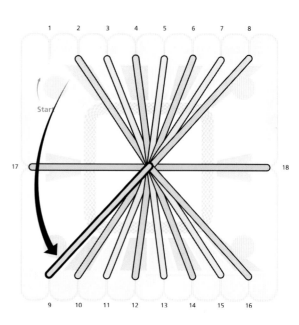

**2.** Center the knot in the hole in the middle of the loom. Take the 2 longest strings and slide them into the notches at the sides (17 and 18). Slide all the other threads into a notch with the matching color. The bottom left notch (9) should be empty.

**3.** Hold your loom so that the START arrow is in the top left corner. Unhook the thread that is in the notch where the START arrow is (1) and hook it into the empty notch in the bottom left corner (9).

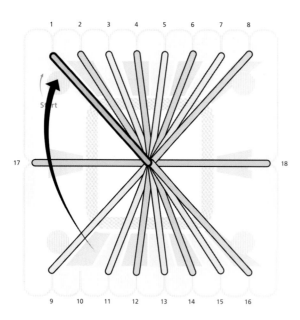

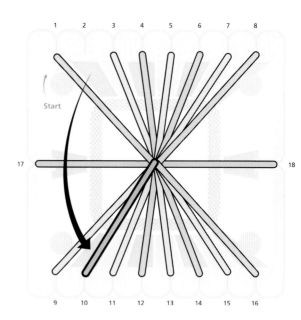

**4.** Unhook the string in notch 10 and hook it into notch 1, which is now empty.

**5.** Move the string from notch 2 down to notch 10.

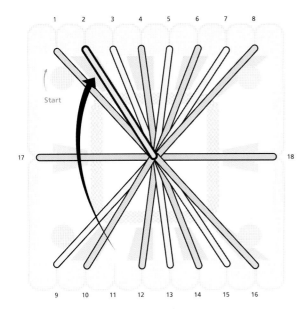

**6.** Move the string from notch 11 up to notch 2.

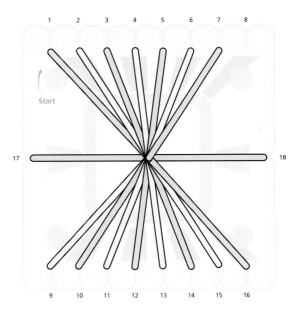

**7.** Continue this way until you have moved all the top strings to the bottom and all the bottom strings to the top. Notch 8 should be empty.

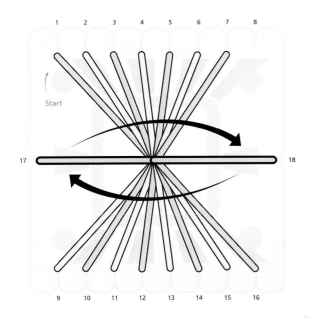

**8.** Unhook the 2 strings at the sides of the loom (17 and 18). Cross the strings over each other and pull them tight, then hook each string into the opposite notch.

**Tip:** It's important to really tighten the side strings well when you cross them over each other. This will bring all the other strings together and make your bracelet the same width all the way through.

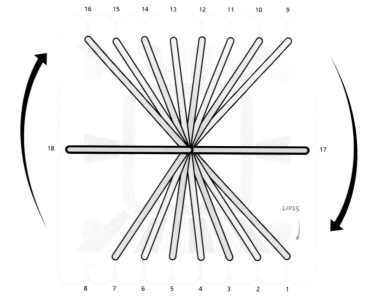

**9.** Rotate the loom until the START arrow is at the bottom right.

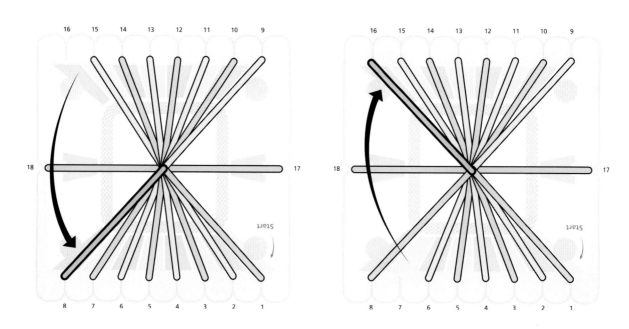

**10.** Move the string from notch 16 down to notch 8.

**11.** Move the string from notch 7 up to notch 16.

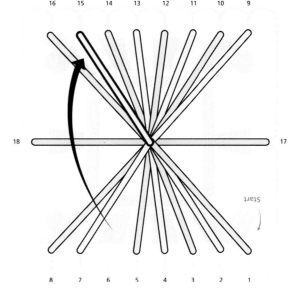

**12.** Move the string from notch 15 down to notch 7.

**13.** Move the string from notch 6 up to notch 15.

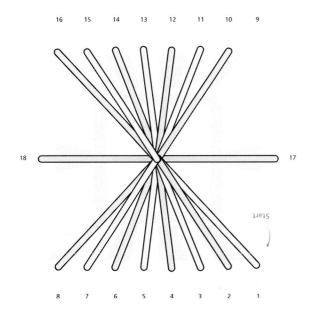

**14.** Continue this way until you have moved all the top strings to the bottom and all the bottom strings to the top. Notch 9 should be empty. Repeat step 8, crossing the 2 strings at the sides over each other.

## To finish your bracelet:

Repeat steps 3–14 until your bracelet is the length you want it to be, and finish off.

**To add beads:** After you complete 5 rows, slide a bead onto the string that is notched into the right side of the loom, before you cross the strings over. Make 5 more rows, then slide a bead onto the string that is notched into the right side of the bracelet maker, before crossing the strings. Repeat the pattern until your bracelet is as long as you want.

cm

0
1
2
3
4
5
6
7
8
9
10
11
12
13
14
15
16
17
18
19
20
21
22
23
24

Bracelet: _____
Made by: _____
Given to: _____
Date: _____
Notes: _____
_____
_____

Bracelet: _____
Made by: _____
Given to: _____
Date: _____
Notes: _____
_____
_____

Bracelet: _____
Made by: _____
Given to: _____
Date: _____
Notes: _____
_____
_____

Bracelet: _____
Made by: _____
Given to: _____
Date: _____
Notes: _____

_____

_____

Bracelet: _____
Made by: _____
Given to: _____
Date: _____
Notes: _____

_____

_____

Bracelet: _____
Made by: _____
Given to: _____
Date: _____
Notes: _____

_____

_____

inches

0

1

2

3

4

5

6

7

8

9

cm
0
1
2
3
4
5
6
7
8
9
10
11
12
13
14
15
16
17
18
19
20
21
22
23
24

Bracelet: _____
Made by: _____
Given to: _____
Date: _____
Notes: _____

_____

_____

Bracelet: _____
Made by: _____
Given to: _____
Date: _____
Notes: _____

_____

_____

Bracelet: _____
Made by: _____
Given to: _____
Date: _____
Notes: _____

_____

_____

Bracelet: _____

Made by: _____

Given to: _____

Date: _____

Notes: _____

_____

_____

Bracelet: _____

Made by: _____

Given to: _____

Date: _____

Notes: _____

_____

_____

Bracelet: _____

Made by: _____

Given to: _____

Date: _____

Notes: _____

_____

_____

inches

0

1

2

3

4

5

6

7

8

9

cm

0
1
2
3
4
5
6
7
8
9
10
11
12
13
14
15
16
17
18
19
20
21
22
23
24

Bracelet: _____
Made by: _____
Given to: _____
Date: _____
Notes: _____

_____

_____

Bracelet: _____
Made by: _____
Given to: _____
Date: _____
Notes: _____

_____

_____

Bracelet: _____
Made by: _____
Given to: _____
Date: _____
Notes: _____

_____

_____

Bracelet: _____
Made by: _____
Given to: _____
Date: _____
Notes: _____
_____
_____

Bracelet: _____
Made by: _____
Given to: _____
Date: _____
Notes: _____
_____
_____

Bracelet: _____
Made by: _____
Given to: _____
Date: _____
Notes: _____
_____
_____

inches

0
1
2
3
4
5
6
7
8
9

cm

0
1
2
3
4
5
6
7
8
9
10
11
12
13
14
15
16
17
18
19
20
21
22
23
24

Bracelet: _____

Made by: _____

Given to: _____

Date: _____

Notes: _____

_____

_____

Bracelet: _____

Made by: _____

Given to: _____

Date: _____

Notes: _____

_____

_____

Bracelet: _____

Made by: _____

Given to: _____

Date: _____

Notes: _____

_____

_____

Bracelet: _____

Made by: _____

Given to: _____

Date: _____

Notes: _____

_____

_____


Bracelet: _____

Made by: _____

Given to: _____

Date: _____

Notes: _____

_____

_____


Bracelet: _____

Made by: _____

Given to: _____

Date: _____

Notes: _____

_____

_____


inches

0

1

2

3

4

5

6

7

8

9

cm

0

1

2

3

4

5

6

7

8

9

10

11

12

13

14

15

16

17

18

19

20

21

22

23

24

Bracelet: _____

Made by: _____

Given to: _____

Date: _____

Notes: _____

_____

_____

Bracelet: _____

Made by: _____

Given to: _____

Date: _____

Notes: _____

_____

_____

Bracelet: _____

Made by: _____

Given to: _____

Date: _____

Notes: _____

_____

_____

Bracelet: _____

Made by: _____

Given to: _____

Date: _____

Notes: _____

_____

_____

Bracelet: _____

Made by: _____

Given to: _____

Date: _____

Notes: _____

_____

_____

Bracelet: _____

Made by: _____

Given to: _____

Date: _____

Notes: _____

_____

_____

inches

0

1

2

3

4

5

6

7

8

9